THE
CALM
COACH

Also in the Pocket Coach series:

THE CONFIDENCE COACH

◆

THE KINDNESS COACH

◆

THE SLEEP COACH

A Pocket Coach

THE
CALM
COACH

DR SARAH JANE ARNOLD

Michael O'Mara Books Limited

First published in Great Britain in 2018 by
Michael O'Mara Books Limited
9 Lion Yard
Tremadoc Road
London SW4 7NQ

A CIP catalogue record for this book is
available from the British Library.

Papers used by Michael O'Mara Books Limited are natural,
recyclable products made from wood grown in sustainable
forests. The manufacturing processes conform to the
environmental regulations of the country of origin.

ISBN: 978-1-78243-915-8 in hardback print format
ISBN: 978-1-78243-013-4 in ebook format

2 3 4 5 6 7 8 9 10

www.mombooks.com
Follow us on Twitter @OMaraBooks

Cover and design by Ana Bjezancevic
Typeset by Amy Lightfoot

Printed and bound in China

This book is dedicated to my clients, past and present, at Brighton Therapy Centre. You amaze me with your strength, teach me through your experiences, and inspire me to learn so that I may offer you more

Thank you for allowing me to be part of your journey, and thank you for helping me in mine

CONTENTS

INTRODUCTION
9

IN TIMES OF STRESS
25

ADOPTING A MINDFUL WAY OF BEING
33

RESPONDING TO YOUR BODY
45

RESPONDING TO YOUR EMOTIONS
55

RESPONDING TO YOUR THOUGHTS
73

RESPONDING BEHAVIOURALLY
93

HELPFUL RESOURCES
125

'The real voyage of
discovery consists not in
seeking new landscapes,
but in having new eyes.'

MARCEL PROUST

INTRODUCTION

Calm. What does this word mean to you? Notice what comes to your mind.

Feeling calm is commonly understood to involve the experience of becoming tranquil; the presence of peaceful feelings and the absence of challenging emotions (or not reacting to them). It's a pleasant, natural state of being that's evoked by our perception of internal and external experiences, and shaped by our thoughts, emotions, body (physiology) and behaviours. Experiencing calm is associated with feelings of peace, serenity – and freedom from agitation or disturbance. When we feel calm we're not lost in anxious thoughts about the future, stuck dwelling on the past, or striving for more in the here and now. Feeling calm involves being fully alive to the present moment, with a non-reactive, non-judgemental and compassionate attitude. It gives the mind and body a much-needed break from the pressures of daily life in our modern world.

When we feel calm, it is associated with our **parasympathetic nervous system**: part of our body's **autonomic nervous system** which regulates automatic/unconscious bodily functions. The (calming) parasympathetic nervous system enables us to rest, digest food, recuperate, relax and soothe our stress reactions. It positively influences our thoughts, increases pleasant emotions and facilitates loving feelings.

Substantial, reliable, research highlights that frequent feelings of calm and physical relaxation are associated with psychological well-being and improved physical health. It's easy to see why the experience of calm is widely considered to be so pleasant and desirable.

◆ UNDERSTANDING STRESS ◆

Stress. It's the antithesis of calm. What comes to mind when you think about experiencing stress?

Like calm, stress is a normal, natural experience. It's a state of psychological and physical strain, evoked by our perception of demanding or adverse circumstances. Our experience of stress is shaped by our thoughts, emotions, physiology and behaviours. Stressors (triggers for stress) can include things like: adjusting to new situations, chronic illness, the emotional, social, financial and physical pressures of everyday life; our attitudes, expectations and beliefs about ourselves, others and the world and our more challenging emotions. If we do not have the resources to cope with these demands – or we believe that we cannot cope with them – then we will feel stressed.

Factors that can help or hinder our ability to cope with stress include our:

- physical health, diet and lifestyle

- relationships and social support

- personality

- ability to relax, and manage our emotions

- planning, prioritizing and time-management skills

- verbal and non-verbal communication style

- past experiences

- capacity for new learning, reflection and self-awareness

- beliefs about ourselves, others and the world

- current focus (being future-focused, present-focused and/or past-focused)

- values and goals

- perception of stress

- belief in our own self-efficacy (our belief in our ability to succeed in specific situations, accomplish tasks, and control our motivation, behaviour and social environment)

- behavioural coping strategies.

Stress is commonly associated with emotions like, frustration, anxiety, helplessness, vulnerability, anger and sadness – all of which can feel really hard to tolerate. We may experience physical symptoms, including a racing heart, headaches, muscle tension and hyperventilation. Stress can make it difficult for us to think slowly, factually, and in a nuanced way about what we need – and want – to do for the best. In an attempt to cope, we often feel reactive urges. It's common for vicious cycles to emerge in times of stress; cycles such as unhelpful interactions between our thoughts, feelings, bodily sensations and reactive coping behaviours.

It can be hard to understand our stress reactions – particularly when they hinder us – but when we consider them from a biological and evolutionary perspective, our natural reactions and inclinations make much more sense. From this point of view, stress is our inbuilt 'threat-detection system' – designed to protect us from things that might harm our well-being. When something physical (such as being chased) or psychological (such as the prospect of rejection) is perceived as a potential threat, the other part of our autonomic nervous system – the **sympathetic nervous system** – automatically gets activated. This bodily system is all about survival and when it gets triggered, it alerts us to the threat and induces temporary physiological changes so that we can fight, flight (run away), or freeze to protect ourselves if we need to. This works well for physical threats, and, if we can bear it, our stress reaction can be a helpful indicator of psychological threats, too.

Unfortunately, it's not only external threats that can activate the sympathetic nervous system. If we perceive them as threatening, then our automatic thoughts, emotions, sensations and urges can activate our (fight/flight/freeze) stress reaction, too. This sets us up to lose a battle that we can't win because, in spite of what we might have been told or what we may wish, we cannot control the occurrence of these internal processes – and we tend to struggle when we try. Self-criticism, trying to suppress challenging thoughts and feelings and struggling with physical pain and sensations are all indications of our fight stress reaction. Avoiding situations that might trigger us and trying to numb ourselves (such as by self-medicating with drugs and alcohol, or sleeping) are common indications of our flight reaction. Feeling numb, overwhelmed, stuck, helpless and tense yet unable to act are indications of our freeze reaction; this can occur if we've tried to fight the stressor and we've tried to avoid it, and neither strategy has worked.

Stress can feel really unpleasant. Numerous research studies tell us that chronic stress is bad for our health because it can cause stress-related physical illnesses and psychological problems. Also, individuals and institutions in Western society can be quick to diagnose human beings with various disorders; doctors prescribe psychiatric drugs to people with the aim of eliminating their symptoms (the difficult thoughts, challenging feelings, sensations and urges associated with stress and past pain). Is there any wonder that our minds will typically judge stress as bad, unwanted and negative? Perhaps your mind made similar judgements earlier, when you were asked to reflect upon the word 'stress'?

▲ ▲ ▲

◆ RESPONDING TO STRESS ◆
– ENABLING CALM

It's not realistic to expect ourselves to feel at peace all of the time. Some emotions will feel pleasant, and they'll easily help us to cultivate a sense of calm (contentment, serenity, love, trust, gratitude). Others, like anxiety, anger, frustration, confusion, shame, disgust, sadness, hurt, helplessness and feeling overwhelmed, can sweep us far away from our wish for peace – *if* we get lost in struggling with them. This, therefore, poses a very real dilemma. When we react to stressors automatically – and experiencing stress is a normal part of being human – how can we adaptively respond to our stress reactions and experience a greater sense of calm in our lives?

▲ ▲▲

◆ YOU CAN ◆

Stress, distress, chronic anxiety, depression, loss, and many other human experiences can leave us feeling as though we have no power – no ability to make changes for ourselves. This belief is reinforced, time and time again, as we repeatedly try to control the things that we cannot actually control. The more we struggle against our automatic internal experiences, the more disempowered we will feel.

With this coach, you can begin to focus your attention and energy on accepting the things that you can't control, and on changing the things that you can. Specifically, it will support you to:

- notice and understand your stress reactions

- cultivate a mindful way of being in response to stress/distress

- respond to your body in a way that helps you

- understand and respond to your emotions in a helpful way

- adaptively respond to your thoughts and urges

- consider the different ways in which you can respond behaviourally to internal and external situations that may be triggering your stress.

The information and techniques within this book are inspired by – and grounded in – Acceptance and Commitment Therapy (ACT), Mindfulness, Dialectical Behaviour Therapy (DBT) and Cognitive Behavioural Therapy (CBT), all of which are proven to facilitate psychological well-being. There are additional recommended resources on page 125.

This book isn't a cure-all for life's troubles. You will still experience stress, and you may forget to use these techniques sometimes. Forgive yourself when you get sucked into old ways of being. It takes time and patience to learn new ways of relating to ourselves and others, but *you can*. You can learn alternative, helpful ways of responding to your thoughts, urges, feelings, bodily sensations and situations. You can strengthen your belief in your ability to cope with stress, and activate your body's parasympathetic nervous system more often. You can enjoy a greater sense of peace and autonomy in daily life, and enable yourself to experience better mental health.

With warm wishes,

Dr Sarah J. Arnold

▲ ▲▲

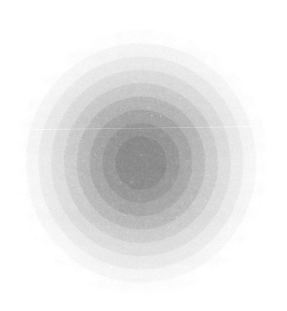

IN TIMES

of

STRESS

'Be curious,
not judgemental.'

WALT WHITMAN

IN TIMES
of
STRESS

◆ NOTICING YOUR STRESS ◆

Common indicators of stress include challenging emotions, difficult thoughts, poor sleep, not exercising, poor diet, social withdrawal, expressions of frustration, and drinking more alcohol than usual. People often report that they stop, or start, doing some things that they don't tend to do when they're feeling more in balance.

What tends to trigger you? Remember, triggers can be internal (challenging emotions, difficult memories, anxious thoughts, physical pain, etc.) or external (demands from others, adjusting to new situations, loss, change, etc.). How do you know when you're feeling stressed?

Noticing is an essential first step towards better self-awareness and positive change. Take some time, at a time that suits you, and reflect upon your personal indicators of stress. Keep a personal notebook nearby as you engage with this book. Making notes about your reflections, feelings, problems and realizations can help to deepen your self-awareness and facilitate positive change.

◆ EXPRESSING YOUR STRESS ◆

Freedom of expression is incredibly important for our well-being – particularly when we're feeling stressed or distressed. The next time you find yourself feeling this way, see if you can release some of what you're holding by writing about it in your notebook – as freely as you can. If you're feeling blocked, or uncertain about how to express yourself, you might find these prompts helpful:

- Describe the situation. What's happened/is happening?

- How does your body feel? Are you experiencing any physical sensations and/or physical pain?

- Note your emotions. How are you feeling?

- Note the thoughts in your mind. What's your mind saying about this situation, others and you?

- Be aware of any automatic behavioural urges. What do you feel like doing right now?

Writing (including creative writing) is just one form of emotional expression that can facilitate cathartic release. Making music, art, art therapy, sand-tray work in therapy and talking therapy are some more examples of expressive activities that you can do and that you might find helpful. It's about finding what's right for you. Different expressive activities will help different people in different ways at different times.

✦ SPOTTING THE STRUGGLE ✦

It's completely natural to try and fight with, take flight from, or freeze when things feel emotionally and physically demanding, threatening and painful. Given our biological make-up and evolutionary past, that makes sense. However, this natural inclination to struggle with our unwanted internal experiences can result in making us feel much worse. The more we try, the louder and stronger our thoughts and feelings can become. This is because our thoughts and feelings are trying to tell us something important about our experience and our needs, and our brain is hard-wired to listen and protect us.

The next time you find yourself hooked into this struggle, see if you can spot it happening in the moment (or as soon after as you can). For example, you might notice yourself wilfully wishing that things would be different from how they are whilst feeling emotionally upset. Recognize your struggle with compassion, and remember – it's completely understandable; stress and distress can feel so challenging.

▲ ▲▲

ADOPTING
a Mindful
WAY OF BEING

'Be kind to yourself ...
You will come to see
that all evolves us.'

RUMI

ADOPTING
a Mindful
WAY OF BEING

It seems counter-intuitive, but one of the first things that we need to do when we notice that we're struggling with stress/distress is to tune in to our struggle and adopt a mindful way of being in response to it. Let's first talk about what mindfulness is, and how you do it, and then we can move to practising it with some simple exercises.

Mindfulness is an ancient practice with Buddhist roots. It's been adopted by Western psychology because a great deal of reliable psychological research has found that practising mindfulness on a regular basis can significantly reduce stress, improve depression and problematic anxiety, and enhance our overall well-being. In essence, mindfulness means tuning in to the present moment, fully and intentionally, with an attitude of compassion, acceptance, non-judgement, openness and curiosity.

Mindfulness can be practised formally (sitting quietly, practising a meditation) and informally (engaging in an activity, such as taking a shower, in a mindful way). When we're being mindful, all internal experiences (thoughts, emotions, urges and bodily sensations) are welcomed and allowed to be – just as they are. Thoughts are viewed as psychological events that may or may not be true; they can be observed as they enter, stay and leave the mind, and we learn to notice when we get lost in their content. Emotions are looked upon as non-threatening messengers that are trying to tell us something about our internal/external experience in a given moment. Physical sensations and urges are noticed in the body without judgement or knee-jerk reactions. If reactions do occur, then they are greeted mindfully. External experiences are managed in much the same way, and we tune in to what we can see, hear, touch, taste and smell – moment by moment. The natural experience of breathing gently is often used as an anchor to help facilitate a sense of internal stability whilst we stay with our experiences in the present moment.

When we're connected to the present moment in this way, we're not struggling with it (not wanting things to be different from how they are, which is a feature of distress). We're not reliving the past (a feature of depression), and we're not caught up in our fears about the future (a feature of anxiety). With time, practise and patience, mindfulness teaches us how to notice our natural reactive tendencies, accept them and respond to them in a way that enhances our well-being.

▲▲▲

◆ PRACTISING MINDFUL ◆
AWARENESS

Find a quiet, comfortable space and just practise mindfully noticing the different facets of your experience right now. Here are some prompts to guide you.

- Mindfully notice your external environment. What colours, shapes and textures do you notice? What do the different surfaces around you feel like when you touch them? What else can you see, hear, touch, taste and smell?

- How does your body feel? Do you notice any sensations, or pains?

- What emotions are you feeling? Use one word for each that you notice (for example, anxiety, gratitude and hopefulness).

- What's your mind thinking about? Mindfully notice your thoughts as they enter your mind, stay, change, leave and perhaps return.

- Are there any behavioural urges? What do you feel like doing or not doing right now? Just notice their presence.

With mindful awareness, you're not trying to change anything. You're simply opening yourself up to what's already there, with a compassionate, curious, open and non-judgemental attitude. This process can help to enhance your self-awareness and acceptance of the present moment.

◆ A MINDFUL MOMENT ◆

When you're noticeably stressed, pause – and take a moment. Spot your struggle with reality, as it is right now. Allow yourself to sit comfortably and quietly in an upright position, and practise the following meditation instead:

1. Take one conscious breath in – and out – and close your eyes.

2. Breathe gently, and tune in to the sensations. Notice how your chest rises and falls, and follow the flow of your breath. Your body and breath are anchors in the ocean of your mind.

3. See if you can allow the sensations, feelings, thoughts and urges that you're experiencing to be here with you now – just as they are.

4. With each breath, you're creating space for your internal experiences. You don't need to like their presence; you're simply acknowledging that they exist in this moment. You're breathing with them.

5. Whenever your mind wanders, greet it with compassion. Acknowledge where it's gone with a short sentence (for example, 'I'm thinking about work'), and then bring the focus of your attention back to the present moment – back to your body; back to your breath.

6. Place your hand on your chest and offer yourself compassion; it can be difficult to sit with our experiences. See if you can be here now, for a few minutes.

7. When you feel ready to finish this short meditation, simply open your eyes.

What was it like to sit with your internal experiences – just for this moment?

▲ ▲ ▲

With this practice, you are nurturing your ability to tolerate the stress/distress that you feel (rather than struggling with it and making things worse). You are anchoring yourself in the present moment, and supporting your mind and body to understand that you're not in any immediate danger – even though you feel emotionally challenged (threatened). You can take the time that you need to understand your stress reaction, and you can choose how you respond to it. Mindfulness supports us to respond to our internal and external experiences with a more self-aware, compassionate and calmer mindset.

▲ ▲ ▲

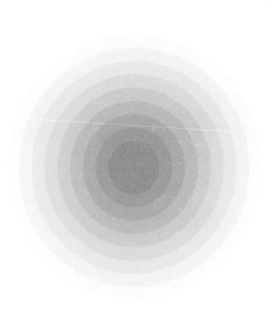

RESPONDING

to

YOUR BODY

'Do you have the patience to
wait until your mud settles
and the water is clear?'

LAO TZU

RESPONDING

to

YOUR BODY

When our stress reaction gets triggered, a number of physiological changes occur. Distress signals activate specific areas of the brain, allowing us to perceive the threat and think fast about how we can reach safety. Stress hormones are released and our blood pressure temporarily increases, helping to fuel our bodies. Our breathing quickens, increasing oxygen to the muscles. Our heart rate increases, circulating oxygen in the blood faster to the muscles, and our muscles tense and contract – ready for action if needed. These reactions, and more, are designed to enable us to protect ourselves from possible danger.

Sometimes, in times of stress, anxiety and panic, we take in too much oxygen and it upsets the natural balance of oxygen and CO_2 (carbon dioxide) in the body. This can cause symptoms such as hyperventilation, pain or a sense of pressure on the chest, sweating, feelings of unreality, dizziness and feeling faint. When this happens, we need to support the body and brain to calm down physically – before we can respond to our stress-related emotions and automatic thoughts in a helpful way.

When you're feeling stress physically, begin by reminding your mind that your stress reaction:

◁ is normal ▷

◁ will pass ▷

◁ is not trying to hurt you ▷

◆ BREATHING FOR CALM ◆

Breathing out for longer than you breathe in helps to restore the body's natural equilibrium (reducing oxygen levels and increasing CO_2 in the lungs). This can help you to feel a little bit calmer. Here's how you do it.

Sit comfortably in an upright position, or stand, and:

Breathe in deeply (inhale) through
your nose for the count of five.

● ● ● ● ●

Hold the breath for a second.

● ● ● ● ●

Breathe out firmly (exhale) through
your mouth for the count of eight.

● ● ● ● ●

Repeat this up to eight times, whilst
counting in your head or on your fingers.

◆ RE-BREATHING FOR PANIC ◆

If you're beginning to hyperventilate, use this technique:

Create a cup with your two hands, as if you were trying to scoop up water, and place this 'cup' over your nose and mouth – creating a seal as much as possible.

● ● ● ● ·

Breathe slowly, as best you can – in through your nose and out through your mouth.

· · · · ● ·

Breathe your exhaled air, like this, no more than ten times.

● ● ● ● ·

Remind yourself that feeling panic is a normal reaction to an abnormally stressful situation. It will pass, and it's not trying to hurt you.

48

This is another effective way to rebalance your oxygen and CO_2 levels – thereby helping your body and brain to calm down.

◆ EXTERNALIZING PHYSICAL ◆ PAIN WITH VISUALIZATION

If you're currently experiencing physical pain, close your eyes and imagine a projection of the pain in front of you:

◀ What shape is it? ▶

◀ What size? ▶

◀ What colour and texture ▶ does it have?

(You can repeat this to distinguish between the different kinds of pain that you're experiencing if needed.)

This exercise can help you to understand, accept and externalize your pain, so that you can gain a little distance from it. When we greet our pain with curiosity, rather than judgement, it can help to reduce the emotional pain that's associated with our physical experience. Be gentle with yourself and practise acceptance, as best you can; struggling with physical pain can make it much worse.

▲▲▲

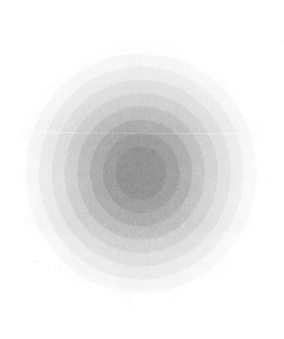

RESPONDING

to

YOUR
EMOTIONS

'When a painful or even a
pleasant feeling arises, the
Truth is – it is there.
Any resistance only causes
more suffering to arise.'

THE VENERABLE
U VIMALARAMSI

RESPONDING

to

YOUR EMOTIONS

Emotions are our messengers. They let us know that something important is going on for us in a given moment. Emotions tell us about our needs and our thoughts; they can motivate us and prepare us to take action; they communicate things to others and evoke others to respond to us; they can warn us about possible threats to our well-being. Here are some examples of universally felt human emotions, and what they may be communicating.

Fear warns us that our mental/physical well-being could be threatened in some way (for example, someone might reject, criticize or dislike us, which could cause emotional pain; we may lose something or someone that we value; we might be in physical danger). Without fear, we would not have survived as a species. We may need to take some form of action to help us effectively manage the perceived threat, and do things that give us a sense of control and mastery.

Sadness often conveys that we've lost something of great importance (for example, a loved one, or our sense of self and autonomy). It can also reflect that our experience of reality doesn't meet our expectations or hopes. Unexpressed anger can often manifest as sadness and be turned in on the self. In response to sadness, we need to be gentle with ourselves and gradually begin doing things that help us to feel confident and competent. We may need to re-learn how to be mindful, how to be assertive, and learn how to problem-solve.

Anger communicates that we've been treated unfairly, or that we believe a situation is wrong and 'should' be different. We may need to be mindful, assertive or problem-solve in response to it – rather than lashing out at ourselves and others.

Happiness is another emotion that comes and goes. It's not a state of being that we can always experience. Happiness typically conveys that our reality matches or is exceeding our expectations; we're being accepted, liked or loved by another/ others, and we're experiencing a sense of pleasure/competence with particular activities. We may want to keep doing the things that evoke this feeling, and think about how else we can experience it.

As you can see, we feel all of our emotions for good reason. Some feel pleasant, and naturally we like them; others can feel very challenging, and understandably we may dislike them. Regrettably, from an early age, many of us are given invalidating messages about our emotions and their expression; you might be familiar with responses such as:

'Don't worry about it'.

'Chin up'.

'Be strong'.

'Don't cry'.

'Be brave'.

'Don't be scared'.

'Pull yourself together'.

'Stop feeling sorry for yourself'.

These messages, and many others, give the impression that we should be happy all the time, we shouldn't feel or express our more challenging emotions – and we should be able to control them. Individuals, society, the media, social media and even some academic literature create and reinforce this message by telling us that we have 'positive' emotions (such as happiness, calm, excitement) and 'negative' emotions (such as anxiety, sadness, frustration, anger, resentment, jealousy). As a result, many of us come to believe that there is something wrong with us if we're feeling sad and anxious; we may begin to view our normal, natural human emotions as unwanted, unmanageable, negative and a sign of personal weakness.

Challenging emotions can certainly *feel* negative, so it makes intuitive sense why we might describe them as negative; they're designed to get our attention, and they can feel really unpleasant and overwhelming. Unfortunately, when we appraise our emotions as negative and unwanted (as we've already discussed), the brain will automatically view them as a threat. This activates our fight/flight/freeze stress reaction (our sympathetic nervous system) and we start struggling against these emotions. We may experience short-term relief with coping strategies like emotional suppression and avoidance, but in the long-term we're liable to feel worse. The emotions invariably come back, louder and stronger, because they are trying to tell us something important about our needs, thoughts and experiences in a given moment. They get triggered, and they will come and go, whether we want them to or not.

Fortunately, managing our own emotions is a skill – and with good teaching, time, self-compassion, patience and practice, this can be learned and mastered. Changing how we think about our emotions – and how we relate to them – is key. Here are some fundamental concepts to reflect upon and practice.

◆ CHANGING YOUR LANGUAGE ◆

Support your mind to understand that your emotions aren't inherently bad, negative or dangerous by calling them 'challenging emotions' – not negative emotions. Challenges are experiences that require effort, patience and perseverance, but they can be managed effectively. Practise this when you think or speak about your own emotions and the emotions of others. Your body may still exhibit a stress reaction with challenging emotions, but adopting this perspective can help to soothe your stress. Remember, the language that we use to describe our experiences shapes our experiences.

UNDERSTANDING ◆ HOW THOUGHTS AND ◆ FEELINGS LINK

Thoughts will evoke feelings, and feelings will trigger thoughts. As a general rule, thoughts typically come to mind as sentences; they reflect our emotions, our perception of a given situation (but not always the facts), our fears, past experiences and beliefs. Feelings, by contrast, are best described using 'feeling words' (i.e. one word for each emotion) such as:

◆ Sad ◆

◆ Anxious ◆

◆ Annoyed ◆

◆ Frightened ◆

◆ Panicky ◆

◆ Happy ◆

◆ Hopeful ◆

See if you can practise noticing the link between your feelings and thoughts when you're experiencing strong, challenging emotions. For example:

I am feeling: overwhelmed, helpless and anxious ... My mind is telling me: 'I can't do this; I can't cope.'

Distinguishing between our feelings and thoughts helps us to understand their impact and respond to them more easily. It's also important because there are some therapeutic tools that we just use for feelings. There are different tools for thoughts, which we'll come to later.

THE 'NAV' TECHNIQUE: ◆ NAVIGATING CHALLENGING ◆ EMOTIONS

It's normal to want stress and distress to go away, but struggling with our emotions does not help. Remember, emotions are our messengers; they let us know that something important is going on for us in a given moment. When we NAV (name, accept and validate) our emotions, it can have several benefits:

1. It can help soothe the emotional reaction that's being triggered. Neuroscientific research confirms that naming our emotions (for example, saying to ourselves, 'I am

feeling anxious' when we're experiencing anxiety) causes the brain to release soothing neurotransmitters which help calm our stress reaction.

2. The brain feels heard. The emotion doesn't need to get louder and stronger in order to convey its message. This contributes to a sense of mental safety and clarity.

3. It creates space for you to decide, with a clearer mind, when and how you want to respond to your emotions.

4. When we're feeling calmer, the mind is more able to think clearly and address the issues that triggered our emotions in the first place.

5. When we accept and validate our emotions, we stop struggling with them. When we stop struggling with them, we're less likely to have emotions about our emotions (for example,

frustration about our anxiety). This helps to reduce the volume and intensity of emotions felt in a given moment.

6. There's a significant body of psychological research which highlights that mindfulness, acceptance, self-compassion and self-validation (features of the NAV technique) are associated with good mental health.

▲ ▲▲

Here's a step-by-step guide to help you navigate your emotions – as and when they arise.

First, pause. Notice that you're emotionally triggered, and take a mindful breath – in and out.

With each emotion that you're feeling now, see if you can:

Name it (using one word for each emotion).For example, I am feeling:

- anxious

- angry

- frustrated

- sad

- overwhelmed.

Accept that this exists for you right now.

Acceptance does not mean liking. You may not want to feel this way, but it's a part of your reality in this moment. You can't control how you're feeling, and you don't need to. Try to breathe with your feelings and the sensations that they bring, making room for them with each breath. Acknowledge them, allow them to be here with you, as best you can. Remember, they're not trying to hurt you – and they will pass.

Validate your feelings.

It is really hard to feel like this. See if you can greet yourself with compassion; try to observe your emotions without judgement. You may understand what's triggered them – you may not. Validate your experience anyway by reminding yourself that you are human, and you're allowed to feel your feelings.

You can practise NAV'ing in your mind, and/or in writing. Whichever feels more helpful for you in the moment.

→ HELP NAMING YOUR EMOTIONS →

If you're not used to naming your emotions, then this may feel unfamiliar and difficult at first. You can use something called a 'Feeling Wheel' if you like. It's an accessible diagram that can help you to identify your emotions with greater ease. See page 125 for one that you can copy and use.

▲▲▲

RESPONDING
to
THOUGHTS

'The greatest weapon
against stress is our ability
to choose one thought
over another.'

WILLIAM JAMES

RESPONDING

to

THOUGHTS

Thoughts (also called cognitions) are psychological events that manifest as words, sentences, images, ideas and memories in the mind. Every day, moment by moment, we experience thoughts that arise automatically and outside of our control about all kinds of things. These **automatic thoughts** are natural reactions to internal and external triggers (for example: other thoughts, emotions, bodily sensations, urges, behaviours and events) and are consciously accessible to our minds. In addition, we all possess attitudes and beliefs that have built up over time as a result of our early lives and past experiences. These may or may not be conscious, but they affect how we think, feel and act, too. Thinking enables us to survive, comprehend the world, develop a sense of self, forge and maintain relationships with others, plan, remember, problem-solve, engage in activities, reflect, imagine, strive, create and thrive.

It's no wonder we tend to listen to our thoughts, believe them and react to them (a process called **fusion**). Fusion is adaptive when the thoughts enable us to live well and cope with life. However, when our thoughts are influenced by stress, fear and old beliefs that may be unkind, unconstructive or untrue – fusing with them can cause us more stress and problems.

Difficult thoughts are a natural part of our human experience and suffering is common. Fortunately, we have the capacity to think about our thinking (a process called **metacognitive awareness**). With this kind of reflection, we can learn to observe our difficult thoughts, 'unhook' ourselves from their content and change our relationship with

74

them (a process called **defusion**), so that we don't inadvertently cause ourselves unnecessary pain and suffering. This can help us feel a greater sense of calm and control during turbulent times.

NOTICING YOUR MIND THINKING THOUGHTS

Thinking is such an innate, automatic and essential process that we may not be aware of ourselves thinking thoughts most of the time. We only tend to notice our thoughts when they become evocative (fear, judgement, disappointment, regret, doubt, nightmares and sorrow).

See if you can practise noticing yourself thinking on a daily basis – when you're not particularly stressed – to get used to the process. For instance:

• Notice your mind thinking specific thoughts. For example, 'I'd like a cup of tea'.

- Notice your mind doing something, like planning. For example, 'What am I going to buy for dinner tonight?'

- Notice what topics your mind is thinking about, too; topics such as work, leisure, friends, or family.

Noticing your mind thinking these thoughts will help you to become more aware of your self-talk and enhance your metacognitive awareness.

▲ ▲ ▲

NOTICING AND NAMING AUTOMATIC-THINKING STYLES

When we get emotionally triggered by an external event (a situation) or an internal event (a thought/feeling/urge/sensation), our thinking will typically change. Over time, automatic-thinking styles can become habitual and detrimental to our well-being if we don't notice them. Here's a list of common ones:

Black-and-white thinking: Seeing only one extreme or another, and not seeing the nuances in between. For example, believing that something or someone is all good or all bad.

Catastrophizing: Fearing and believing that a situation is far worse than it actually is in reality. It's common to imagine and predict that the worst outcome will definitely happen.

Comparisons: Negatively comparing ourselves to

others. For example, thinking that we're not as good or as capable or as attractive as they are.

Emotional reasoning: Viewing ourselves or the situation based upon how we're feeling. For example, 'I feel scared; something bad is going to happen'.

Empty positive thinking: Attempting to reassure ourselves with phrases like 'It'll be fine', which we don't really believe. This can unintentionally invalidate our emotions and interfere with our ability to manage internal/external situations effectively because it encourages us to ignore what's bothering us.

Filtering: Focusing on the difficult/unwanted aspects of a given situation – forgetting to consider the pleasant parts and the bigger picture.

Jumping to conclusions: Making assumptions, judgements and predictions about someone or a situation, without knowing all of the relevant facts first, and reaching unwarranted conclusions. We might assume that we know what someone else is thinking or why they behave in a particular way.

Mood-dependent retrieval: Having thoughts that match with our current mood and emotion/s. For example, we're more likely to recall depressive memories of sad times and losses when we're feeling sad, and more likely to recall pleasant thoughts and memories when we're contented.

Over-generalizing: Making inaccurate generalized statements about how things are. For example, something will occur and the mind will say 'this always happens'. In reality – it may happen a lot, or it may not happen a lot, but it doesn't *always* happen – there are exceptions.

Personalizing: Regularly relating things back to ourselves; often blaming ourselves for things that go wrong or could go wrong – even though we're not responsible or only partly responsible for the outcome.

Ruminating: Worrying over and over again about a particular concern or fear. Often the mind is trying to solve a perceived problem, but it's got stuck in a loop without finding a workable solution.

Self-critical voice/Internalized bully: Putting ourselves down, criticizing and bullying ourselves. For example, we might label ourselves as 'stupid', 'worthless' or 'useless'.

Shoulds: Regularly thinking or saying 'I should', 'they should've', 'you should', etc., can put unreasonable demands and pressure on ourselves and others, creating unrealistic, unachievable standards and expectations.

Make a note of which of these automatic-thinking styles resonate with you.

Most of us will experience some or all of these styles of thinking from time-to-time. They're a natural consequence of:

- the way our minds work

- stress and fear

- past pain and past experiences.

For example, mood-dependent retrieval is a normal, natural psychological phenomenon. When a memory is formed (encoded), it's easier to retrieve/recall it when our current mood matches how we felt when the memory was first encoded. Unfortunately, this can cause us a great deal of distress when mood-matching memories of past pain get triggered on top of how we're feeling in the present. It's a really difficult part of being human.

Jumping to conclusions is a common reaction to stress and fear. In times of uncertainty, the mind will automatically seek a sense of safety and certainty. Because life can be uncertain, and we cannot control this, the mind will sometimes make negative predictions about situations in

order to try and gain some sense of certainty –
even if the prediction isn't true or desirable.

The self-critical voice is a thinking style that's
common for people who've been bullied, judged,
invalidated or criticized by others. We internalize
(absorb) our experiences with our parents, peers,
partners, etc., and consciously/unconsciously
conclude that we're being treated this way
because we're unworthy, unlovable or stupid.
Even if the abuse stops, we may continue to be
unkind to ourselves because, on some level, we
think that it's what we deserve.

Fortunately, we can begin to disentangle ourselves
from our stress-related thoughts – and reduce
their impact – by noticing and naming them, as
and when they arise. Here's how:

1. **Tune in to your thinking as soon as you notice
   any strong challenging emotions or stress-
   related bodily sensations.**

2. See if you can notice what your mind is telling you. What thoughts are popping into your mind?

3. With a mindful attitude, name any automatic-thinking styles in your thoughts. For example, you can respond by saying, 'That's over-generalizing', or 'Hello, self-critical voice'.

With this awareness, the thoughts are less likely to unconsciously influence you in an unhelpful way. What's more, you can then choose to continue with what you were doing, or address the issue/s arising in your thoughts – in a more grounded way.

▲ ▲ ▲

◆ THOUGHT DEFUSION ◆ CONTINUED

Here are some more defusion techniques that you can try.

Mindful appreciation of your mind

Anxious thoughts are the mind's way of trying to protect you from possible harm. Remind yourself of this next time you experience them, and see if you can appreciate their function; your brain is trying it's best to keep you safe. You don't have to buy in to the thoughts. You can decide for yourself what you do and don't do, based upon how you want to behave as a person.

Identifying the voice of past pain and/or fear

Naturally, because of our past experiences, we come to believe particular things about ourselves, others and the world. Sometimes these beliefs help us ('I'm lovable'); other times they can hinder us ('I'm useless'). The next time you notice a belief that hinders you, see if you can see it for what it is – a reflection of fear and/or past pain that's built up into a story that you tell yourself and have come to believe. Then, name it: 'That's my past pain talking' or 'That's fear talking'.

Describing your thoughts

See if you can put the following phrase in front of your thoughts when you get emotionally triggered: 'I'm having a thought that ... [describe the thought].' For example: 'I'm having thoughts that she doesn't like me anymore'. This simple technique can help your mind to remember that it is thinking thoughts and they may not be 100% true or helpful. If they are true, then you can think about what might help you or the situation when you're ready to.

▲ ▲ ▲

→ NOTICE YOUR LANGUAGE ←

The language that we use, in our thoughts and in our speech, influences how we think, feel, act and interact. Consider the difference between the stress-related automatic thought: 'I can't cope', and the alternative thought: 'I'm feeling overwhelmed and I'm finding it really hard to cope'. The former suggests that the individual can't help themselves; it may prompt them to behave in ways that will unwittingly reinforce this belief.

Now consider the alternative thought. Notice how this language reflects the individual's reality, clearly and accurately, but in a way that opens up space for autonomy and coping. See if you can notice your language when you're feeling triggered, and adjust it as required.

▲ ▲ ▲

◆ QUESTION: IS IT HELPFUL? ◆

As you know, when we get emotionally triggered, our thoughts can become reactive and unconstructive. The next time you notice this happening, you might find it helpful to ask yourself one or more of the following questions:

- Does it help me to fuse with this thought?

- How would I act if I believed these thoughts? How might I act if I didn't believe them?

- What would a self-compassionate response be?

- What would I say to a close friend if they were facing this situation or having these thoughts?

▲ ▲▲

RESPONDING
BEHAVIOURALLY

'Be resolutely and faithfully
what you are; be humbly
what you aspire to be.'

HENRY DAVID THOREAU

RESPONDING BEHAVIOURALLY

In times of stress and distress, you *can* control what you do and don't do. You might find it helpful to ask yourself the following questions in challenging times:

- What can I do to help myself or this situation?

- How can I best take care of myself right now?

- What do I need?

What you choose to do will naturally depend upon your wants, needs and the situation. In this section, we'll explore some behavioural self-help tools that can enable calm and help you to support your own well-being.

LEARNING TO COMFORT YOURSELF

Choosing to comfort yourself in an adaptive way (also known as 'self-soothing') can really help to stabilize your mind. Self-soothing involves being gentle, comforting, peace-making and compassionate with yourself, through activities that feel nurturing and calming. This can improve the moment that you're in, and help you to tolerate the pain and distress that you're feeling without making things worse. It can help you to respond to your emotions thoughtfully, rather than reacting to them impulsively. The intention is not to get rid of them; you're simply recognizing that they exist, and you're choosing to respond to yourself with kind-heartedness.

You may or may not know what kinds of things help to bring you a sense of comfort during times of stress and distress. Sometimes it takes a while to figure these things out – and that's okay. It can be helpful to think about activities that will nourish you in some way and appeal to your senses. For example, what comforting things might you like to see, hear, touch, taste and smell?

Here are examples of some activities that you can try when you next feel the need for some comfort and care:

- Watching videos of heart-warming things on the internet.

- Reading or watching documentaries about inspiring people, places and things.

- Lighting candles.

- Calming, coloured lights.

- Mindfully listening to comforting music.

- Mindfully applying a natural, beautifully scented hand lotion.

- Taking a warm bath or shower mindfully, with scents that you enjoy and soft lighting.

- Wearing your favourite, comfortable (and comforting) items of clothing.

- Placing your hand on your chest, and wishing yourself well.

- Using an aromatherapy burner with natural essential oils for relaxation.

- The smell and taste of a (non-alcoholic) drink that you enjoy.

- Intentionally watching your favourite television series or film in a warm and cozy environment.

- Adult colouring in a comfortable, calming setting.

You may notice an urge to soothe yourself in a way that's counter-productive (binge-eating junk food; drinking excessive amounts of alcohol; spending money that you'd rather have saved). These escapist ways of managing stress and distress can be very addictive because they actually work in the short-term (they temporarily reduce the challenging feelings). However, they tend to create more problems in the long-term and can leave you feeling worse.

You may notice some resistance when you plan to engage in helpful forms of self-care. Doing things differently, helping yourself and allowing yourself to feel good may feel unfamiliar and a little scary. This is completely normal. Appreciate your mind's hesitation, and do it anyway. You deserve to spend your time mindfully, engaging with ways of being that add value to your life and truly nurture you! You can choose how you want to restore your psychological equilibrium, and you can behave like the person that you want to be.

◆ 'WHAT'S ON YOUR MIND' ◆

This technique can help you to recognize – and effectively respond to – the different things that may be on your mind when you're feeling overwhelmed and stressed.

▼ ▼ ▼

1. Take an A4 piece of paper and write in the centre: 'What's on my mind?'

2. In no particular order, write down everything that comes to mind.

3. Now, take a moment and look at what's on your piece of paper.

▲ ▲ ▲

Writing it down can help you experience a little distance from it all. What's more, it can help you to see (and compassionately understand) why you're feeling so overwhelmed. From here, you can creatively respond to what's on your mind in a more logical way. For instance, there may be lots of outstanding tasks contributing to your stress.

Purchase a page-per-day diary; reflect upon what's essential, and what's simply desirable. Highlight them on your piece of paper (for example, orange means essential – green means desirable), and then systematically add them into your diary (for the day/week/month). Create plans for yourself that feel achievable, and focus on completing the essential things first. Don't forget to schedule in pleasurable activities, because they're essential for your well-being, too.

▲ ▲ ▲

PRACTICAL PROBLEM-SOLVING

Practical problem-solving is a helpful way of dealing with practical worries that affect us and which we can do something about. This can help us experience a greater sense of calm because we're supporting the mind to know that it can cope. Here's how you do it:

1. Clearly identify the problem (in your notebook).

2. Adopt an open, non-judgemental attitude and brainstorm all the possible things that you can do in response to the problem. Write down your options, and then consider the pros and cons of each.

3. Choose your approach to the problem, and

identify the steps that you'll need to take in order to make this happen.

4. Check that each step in your plan is realistic and achievable, and begin when you're ready.

5. Offer yourself some genuine personal praise for addressing this. Now you have a plan to deal with the situation.

▲ ▲ ▲

◆ BEFRIENDING YOUR ANXIETY ◆

You can take a similar approach with anxiety when it arises. Anxiety is maintained when we overestimate the threat, and underestimate our ability to cope. When we're feeling overwhelmed, uncertain, anxious and helpless, we're prone to believing that we can't cope because that's how it *feels* – we're struggling to cope. Again with a notepad, you can combat this with the following anxiety-management strategy:

▼▼▼

1. First, ask yourself, 'what am I anxious about?' Try to be as realistic as possible, and write it down.

2. Say this does happen, how could you cope with it? What can you do to help yourself and the situation? Patiently give yourself time to reflect upon this, and write down your ideas and options.

3. Notice what happens to your anxiety when you befriend it, gently, and decide how you can help yourself and the situation.

▲▲▲

◆ ASSERTIVENESS TRAINING ◆

We are born with the capacity to be assertive. When a newborn baby wants, needs or feels something, it cries out to get its needs met. As we get older, and life gets more complicated, we can find it hard to express what we think, feel and need. We might be reluctant to express ourselves because of feared consequences. We might have learned to communicate in passive or aggressive – or passive-aggressive – ways, because that's what has worked, or because that's how our parents or partners have communicated. Over the years, it's easy to forget our basic human rights. Remembering these rights, and practising behaving in line with them, can help you to find your assertive voice once more:

- **I am allowed to feel my feelings.**

- **I am allowed to respectfully express my opinions and beliefs if I want to.**

- I have the right to be listened to.

- My thoughts and feelings matter, even if others don't agree with them.

- I am allowed to change my mind.

- I am allowed to say that I don't understand.

- I am allowed to make mistakes, and I can learn to own them when they happen.

- I can choose to say 'yes', and 'no', for myself.

- I can set my own boundaries, according to what feels comfortable for me.

- I can choose to behave in a manner that respects the rights of others and myself.

- I am allowed to walk away from situations and people that harm my well-being.

Being assertive can help to improve our relationships with others and ourselves. It doesn't necessarily mean that we'll get our needs met or our voices heard, but it gives us the best chance. So what might assertiveness look like, behaviourally, in practice? Here are some pointers:

- Pause, take a mindful breath, and try to verbally express what you think, feel and need in a way that's respectful of both yourself and the person/people that you're talking to.

- Hold your head up, and do your best to speak clearly and concisely.

- Keep your voice at a constructive volume (not too loud; not too soft).

- Offer the other person your eye contact.

- Be sincere.

- Acknowledge the other person's point of view.

- Empathize with them, as appropriate.

- Use 'I' statements: 'I think ...' – 'I would like to ...' – 'I agree ...' – 'I disagree ...'.

- Highlight your own experience, without blaming the other person. So, for example, 'When you ... shout at me, I feel ... really upset and anxious.' This is far better than saying to someone that they've made you feel a certain way, as this can sound blaming and evoke defensiveness in the other person.

- Speak your process. For example, instead of being silent, explain that you're not sure what to say right now. This will help the other person to understand your internal world and reduce the likelihood of misunderstandings.

- Check in with the other person. For example, 'What do you think about ..?' – 'What are your thoughts about ...?' Demonstrate that you're wanting to listen and co-operate.

- Disarm criticism by owning it (if it's true), rather than becoming defensive. For example, 'Yes, I can be messy – you're right'.

- Respectfully disagree when necessary. For example, 'I disagree, but you're entitled to your opinion'.

- You can notice your emotions and express them verbally, rather than acting them out behaviourally. For example, you can choose to say 'I feel really angry with you' rather than shouting at the person, slamming doors, or breaking things.

- If you're unable to contain your emotions, then explain that you need to take some time to calm down. If you hope to be able to talk again later, say so.

Many people report feeling scared that being assertive will get them in trouble with people or damage their bonds. In actuality, what people tend to find (and psychological research supports this) is that when they speak openly and honestly with others, in a kind and respectful way, they tend to (a) experience improvements in their bonds, and (b) get their needs met more often than when they are passive, aggressive or passive-aggressive.

Learning how to be more assertive can significantly improve your quality of life, decrease depression and reduce problematic anxiety. Try it and see for yourself! Do please be patient with yourself, though. When you've been communicating in a non-assertive way for a sustained period of time, it takes a while to re-learn how to be assertive; keep practising.

◆ PHYSICAL SELF CARE ◆

Sleep: Getting enough good-quality sleep (around eight hours per night) supports the mind and body to feel calmer. Of course, it's not always easy to sleep well. If poor sleep is a problem for you, consider purchasing some self-help books initially (see page 126 for some recommended resources). If it remains a problem, consider seeing a psychologist who specializes in helping people with sleep problems.

Diet: There's a great deal of solid scientific research which highlights the relationship between a healthy balanced diet (rich in fruits, vegetables, protein and whole grains) and good mental health. You can make this choice for yourself on a daily basis, and you can do it on a budget if necessary. Remind yourself to drink enough water, as dehydration makes stress management that much harder. Reduce your consumption of alcohol and avoid recreational drugs that will artificially alter your mood. They'll deprive you of the chance to realize that you can learn how to cope with your stress and distress without them.

Exercise: Find a form of exercise that you actually like, rather than trying to force yourself to do something that you don't enjoy. Some people love going to the gym, but there are many other enjoyable and fun ways to keep fit. Here are a few of them:

- Dancing.

- Yoga (different kinds of yoga suit different people).

- Pilates.

- Jogging/running.

- Walking in nature.

- Cycling.

- Home workout videos.

- Martial arts.

- Walking from A to B instead of taking the car or public transport.

- Swimming.

- Trampolining.

- Indoor and outdoor rock-climbing.

Finding a form of exercise that you can do, and enjoy, on a regular basis can significantly reduce your stress levels and support you to feel more calm, confident and competent.

▲ ▲ ▲

◆ MINDFULNESS MEDITATION ◆ PRACTICE

Formal mindfulness meditation is an invaluable activity to practise, both on a daily basis and when we're feeling stressed. Reliable psychological research highlights that regular mindfulness meditation can enhance metacognitive awareness, self-insight, gratitude, stress and emotion management, relationship satisfaction, social connection, self-compassion, compassion towards others and immune-system functioning. It's also been found to decrease anxiety, stress, self-criticism, emotional reactivity, obsessive-compulsive symptoms, and prevent depression relapses. As you can see, there are many ways in which mindfulness practice can enable us to experience a greater sense of calm.

If you're keen to learn more, the helpful resources section at the back of this book will offer you some excellent preliminary texts and a link to some great, guided meditations. Reading, joining a mindfulness meditation group, practising at home (with guided meditations), attending a Mindfulness-Based Stress Reduction course (MBSR) or Mindfulness-Based Cognitive Therapy programme (MBCT) are all great ways to develop the skill of mindfulness.

◆ VALUE-BASED LIVING ◆

Your values are ongoing principles and ways of being that reflect who you are and want to be, rather than goals to be completed. Psychological research tells us that knowing what our values are – and living life in accordance with them – can really enhance our well-being. Many people report an increased sense of personal fulfillment, autonomy and emotional stability as a consequence of practising value-based action.

Take some time, at a time that suits you, and reflect upon your values. They may be things that you currently embody and practice, or they may be things that deeply matter to you, but are not currently reflected in your way of being. They are still your values, and you can align yourself with them – more and more – with time, a mindful attitude and practice.

You might find it helpful to ask yourself some or all of the following questions and note your responses:

- What really matters to me as a person?

- How do I want to treat myself, others and the world around me?

- What personal qualities do I want to cultivate?

▲▲▲

Here's a list of some core values that people hold, which may help you to clarify yours:

◆ Friendship ◆

◆ Reliability ◆

◆ Respect ◆

◆ Forgiveness ◆

◆ Fun ◆

◆ Control ◆

◆ Beauty ◆

◆ Friendliness ◆

◆ Authenticity ◆

◆ Bravery ◆

◆ Acceptance ◆

◆ Activity ◆

◆ Freedom ◆

◆ Reciprocity ◆

◆ Adaptability ◆

◆ Patience ◆

◆ Personal growth ◆

◆ Self Respect ◆

◆ Adventure ◆

◆ Assertiveness ◆

◆ Community ◆

◆ Connection ◆

◆ Autonomy ◆

◆ Caring ◆

◆ Charity ◆

◆ Determination ◆

◆ Dependability ◆

◆ Contribution ◆

◆ Discipline ◆

◆ Gratitude ◆

◆ Excitement ◆

◆ Fairness ◆

◆ Challenge ◆

◆ Commitment ◆

◆ Fitness ◆

◆ Cooperation ◆

◆ Creativity ◆

◆ Willpower ◆

◆ Wisdom ◆

◆ Self-compassion ◆

◆ Compassion ◆

◆ Curiosity ◆

◆ Generosity ◆

◆ Hard work ◆

◆ Empathy ◆

◆ Encouragement ◆

◆ Honesty ◆

◆ Self-care ◆

◆ Loyalty ◆

◆ Self-respect ◆

◆ Effectiveness ◆

◆ Equality ◆

◆ Love ◆

◆ Order ◆

◆ Openness ◆

◆ Humility ◆

◆ Humour ◆

◆ Intimacy ◆

◆ Justice ◆

◆ Kindness ◆

◆ Sensuality ◆

◆ Romance ◆

◆ Sexuality ◆

◆ Knowledge ◆

◆ Learning ◆

◆ Skillfulness ◆

◆ Supportiveness ◆

◆ Listening ◆

◆ Meaningful work ◆

◆ Mindfulness ◆

◆ Non-judgement ◆

◆ Open-mindedness ◆

◆ Safety ◆

◆ Security ◆

◆ Pleasure ◆

◆ Proactivity ◆

◆ Quiet time ◆

◆ Responsibility ◆

◆ Spirituality ◆

◆ Stability ◆

◆ Trust ◆

◆ Rest and relaxation ◆

▲ ▲ ▲

Make a note of the values that are most important to you right now, and reflect upon what you can do to help yourself live in line with them. For example:

Self-awareness (value): I will commit to practising a guided mindfulness meditation every evening for one week (action).

Humour and friendship (values): I will research recommended comedy films and arrange times to watch them with friends (action).

Self-care (value): I will practise NAV'ing my emotions and self-soothing for the next week – and reflect upon this in my notebook (action).

Ultimately, you can craft a life for yourself that you want to live. The smallest, value-based changes can make a big difference. Over time, they add up and create significant positive change. Step by step, you can explore and practise the techniques and ways of being outlined in this coach – and discover what best benefits you.

This will help you to develop confidence in your ability to cope with life's challenges – and enjoy a greater sense of calm.

▲ ▲ ▲

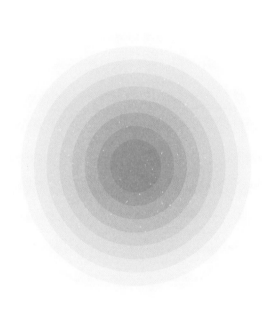

HELPFUL
RESOURCES

HELPFUL
RESOURCES

Acceptance and Commitment Therapy
www.thehappinesstrap.com

Assertiveness training
(The Centre for Clinical Interventions)
www.cci.health.wa.gov.au

Enhancing metacognitive awareness
Siegal, D. *Mindsight: Transform Your Brain with the New Science of Kindness*. Oneworld Publications, 2011.

Guided mindfulness meditations
franticworld.com/free-meditations-from-mindfulness

Help naming your emotions
https://themighty.com/2018/11/i-feel-nothing-wheel-of-emotions/

How to deal with a difficult dilemma
www.actmindfully.com.au/upimages/10_Steps_For_
Any_Dilemma.pdf

Introductory texts about mindfulness
Alidina, S. *Mindfulness for Dummies*. John Wiley &
Sons Ltd, 2010.

Arnold, Dr S J. *The Mindfulness Companion*. Michael
O'Mara Books, 2016.

Kabat-Zinn, J. *Wherever You Go, There You Are:
Mindfulness Meditation for Everyday Life*. Hyperion
Books, 1994.

Penman, D. and Williams, M. *Mindfulness: A Practical
Guide to Finding Peace in a Frantic World*. Hachette
Digital, Little Brown Book Group, 2011.

Williams, M., Teasdale, J., Segal, Z., and Kabat-Zinn,
J. *The Mindful Way through Depression: Freeing Yourself
from Chronic Unhappiness*. The Guilford Press, 2007.

Living well with physical pain
Kabat-Zinn, J. *Full Catastrophe Living: How to
Cope with Stress, Pain and Illness using Mindfulness
Meditation*. Revised edition. Piatkus, 2013.

HELPFUL RESOURCES

Mindfulness resources from world-renowned
professionals
www.themindfulnesssummit.com

Responding to addictive urges
www.portlandpsychotherapyclinic.com/2011/11/
riding-wave-using-mindfulness-help-cope-urges

Responding to sleep problems
Arnold, Dr S J. *The Can't Sleep Colouring Journal*.
Michael O'Mara Books, 2016.

Arnold, Dr S J. *The Sleep Coach*. Michael O'Mara
Books, 2018.

Meadows, Dr G. *The Sleep Book: How to Sleep Well
Every Night*. Orion, 2014.

www.howsleepworks.com/hygiene.html

'Safe Room' Visualization technique for creating
calm
donnabutler.bandcamp.com/releases

▲▲▲

ABOUT THE AUTHOR

Dr Sarah Jane Arnold is a Chartered Counselling Psychologist and author. She works in private practice, offering integrative psychological therapy that is tailored to the individual. She supports her clients to understand their pain, break free from limiting vicious cycles, and respond adaptively to difficult thoughts and challenging feelings so that they can live a full and meaningful life.

Sarah lives in Brighton (UK) with her partner Mine, their dog Oprah, Priscilla the bearded dragon, and her guinea pigs Jack and Basil.

You can find Sarah at:
www.themindfulpsychologist.co.uk
www.instagram.com/themindfulpsychologist

▲ ▲ ▲